# Sticks

## Timothy Robbins

**Cyberwit.net**
HIG 45 Kaushambi Kunj, Kalindipuram
Allahabad - 211011 (U.P.) India
http://www.cyberwit.net
Tel: +(91) 9415091004
E-mail: info@cyberwit.net



Printed at Repro India Limited.

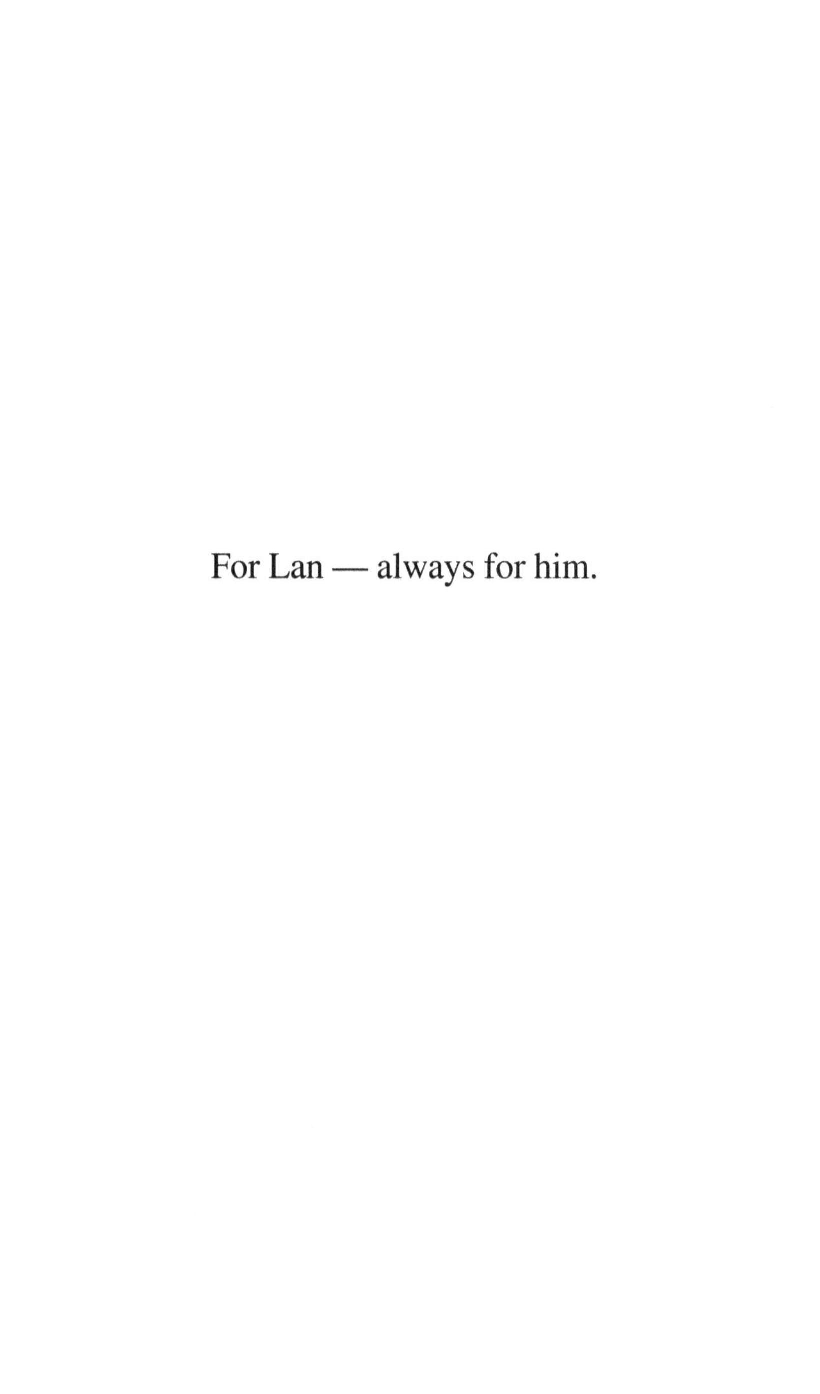

For Lan — always for him.

# Contents

# Sticks

1.
The face in my tea won't look me in the eye.

I write the manifesto on my lips and transfer it to yours.

I blow on the soup, confident it won't blow on me, assuming it would blow in vain if it did.

Every stick figure bears a full moon head.


2.
Prodded by my breath, the lake shivers — Clouds somersault.

If you catch me alive you catch me in a lie.

I'm your sneeze — You can't resist me.

I used to think the head in 'head cleaner' was the head on our shoulders.

So many reasons to clean even the cleanest of heads!

Keigo naked in bed — a dream so brief I don't see him breathe.

Why do I assume he's not dead?

3.

Kids with sunburned arms relieve each other at the ice cream crank.

Remove this stick lest someone whack you with it.

A few words on the radio — hard to hear over the shower — the threat of peace — hard to hear over every species of child scream.

Simple time? — Simplified time? — Which should I isolate?

Kids with new groins and too many scoops on their paper plates.

The more I languish in the heat, the less I languish in heat.


4.

There should have been a third tree — a Tree of Forgiveness — The need for that tree drove us from the garden.

What do you do when your supervisor confides that her father engendered in her five split personalities — all of them children?

I picture President Wilson, stymied before his typewriter — three days and nights, agonizing over his riposte to the Kaiser re: the Lusitania — refusing to hear details lest they enrage him.

The typewriter schemes to supplant the First Lady — to undermine the seating chart she devised so artfully.


5.

Tea sings in my veins — a nerve-wracking pleasure.

One could handily get lost in this seating chart.

My date talks about his survival course and the time he ate a seagull.

He hints at his surveillance training — I wonder if he's using it now.

It wasn't like a divorce, which allows us time to adjust — It wasn't like an amputation, for which we are anesthetized —

It reminded me of a kid in my hometown who went joyriding with his arm bobbing out the window as though he were signaling a right turn for the driver when a guy wire sliced off  his forearm.

We plant the tree ourselves — Guy wires water it with selfless blood.

I was a martyr to Acne — acne, one of the harsh religions — My friend's grandmother was sure I'd been "beaten with the Ugly Stick."


6.
I prayed the light in his eyes wasn't fever.

I should have foreseen his wanting me to leave the instant he came — I felt the same at his age.

His hands are the masters of that jumbo cup.

Eight sticks and two thumbs up — stick out like sore dicks.

He stretches — horizon's first light between his belt and the hem of his shirt.

It reminded him of his time in the MRI machine — It was like
being in that box on top of someone — two beauties that didn't
succumb to the evil fairy's cradle song while the hospital
personnel slumped and slept.


7.
We keep forgetting there's no Autumn here.

I take up my work where you left off.

A cross resting in withered cleavage — Someone believes —
Someone prays to me.

"Night," he says, "is the shadow I cast."

"No," I counter, "it's the light I retract."

My brother and I play Ker Plunk — I think of knitting needles
and Excalibur — I want to feel like a marble waiting to fall —
falling —


8.
"One woman is wed to my future — When I lust for the wrong
bride, the ground quakes."

Thus spake my schizophrenic friend on Kirkwood when his meds
befriended him with brief respite.

Ockeghem's *Missa Prolationum*, whispering like a happy
confession from our stereo, is meant to wed our sleep — My
dreaming brain amplifies the mass and places it in the mouths
of militant monks — marching up and down our street — around
our house while we crawl on our bellies from room to room in
search of a spot no window can espy.

9.
Black, black, black are the bruises blooming on my true love's arms.

At sixteen it's easy to think being happy is beside the point.

When the newborn declined to breathe, the matriarch, seeing an affront to her authority,  urged him as she would hit an elephant that balked at kneeling or a servant who burned the rice.

That newborn was shuttled across the globe — The plan was to lay him in my arms like the Christ child.

By the time his family got here, he was a young man, his own man, and mine.

10.
If you're gentle, it's no use trying to be brutal — even if that's what the other guy craves.

I envy amphibians, the sly way they absorb oxygen with their whole skin.

Of course he knows if he stints on the lube the condom will break and he'll get what I deny him.

And I'll get what I deny him.


11.
When Sunny stood six, any dragonfly she stunned would be stripped of its wings, any frog would be boiled alive.

Now she's 32 — Her father is brokering a marriage for her to stop millions of yen from going to Granddad's bastards.

Her family bribes her with an SUV so she can drive the few blocks to school without being mauled by a Rottweiler.

Hoping to make her laugh, I start the tale about my female students at Jerry's Deli gauging each other's breasts across the table at Thanksgiving dinner.

Just in time, I remember she has given herself a mastectomy.

Doubting, Thomas barely touches the opening, afraid of being right, afraid of being wrong, afraid of inspiring the wound.

I slip my fingers all the way in to stop it from closing.

12.
Morrison shakes his wilted lily at the cops — Cops answer with nightsticks dangling from loops.

Was he a shaman or a sham — a pole dancer — a common street corner flasher?

Was it Manson and his girl prancers who broke on through?

The older yardsticks — old apple-flesh brown — had more wood than the new yellow, orange and pink gifts from the only bank in town.

In the art room there was lots of leaning across heavy white wheel-shaped tables —

Razor blades in utility knives moved along the edges of metal

yardsticks — It took concentrated pressure and multiple passes
— Sometimes a tender lock of cardboard matting curled up from
the cutting.


13.
Jeff wants me to get a head start on old age's whittling down to a
few essential anecdotes.

Woven through time — red white and blue strips of crêpe paper
— 4th of July spokes.

Should I also put a rush on wrinkles and liver spots?

Long before texting flourished I knew my mom would be a great
texter — Our minds would meet on opposite ends of possibility.

A plank secretly hoping to sink — hoping to be taken up by a
pirate ship — hoping to grow foot by foot, a weird parody of an
erection — a mutineer shuffling toward the plank's edge.


14.
The essential songs are airy as a bird's cage — The five-note
song of the mourning dove is one.

A week before Good Friday sirens come for the unwed
madonnas of Catharine Ferguson Academy.

90 per cent attendance, 97 per cent graduation, an urban farm in
the backyard, preschool education for their children — hardly the
usual benefits for teenage mothers.

These virtues were rendered moot by one deadly sin — No one
was making a profit.


15.
The former old high school where I grew through 5th and 6th
grades has been converted to low-income housing.

A couple quarrels where Miss Tilton tried to excuse a boy from
board-work without drawing attention to the living sock in his
crotch that necessitated the excusing.

This made my twelve-year-old self sad and empathetic, so I
learned to associate desire with pity.

Love hung — swung from Miss Tilton with her glasses.

Someone watches a Netflix original in the science room where I
watered every classmate's plant except the one that belonged to
the girl who danced with the boy I wanted to dance with.

Someone struggles with her hair where Joel Womack used to
fiddle dreamily with his yellow cowlick.

Someone bases their genocidal fantasies on Revelation in the
cafeteria-gym where my fifth-grade teacher shot baskets after
school and made me (I was too mild to protest) rebound.


16.
In little time a high chainlink fence evolves into a high hirsute
hedge — a playground into a parking lot.

I want to live in a trailer — a house susceptible to rust — a
worthy opponent of trust.

These are not fantasies — I'm not turned on — This swelling is
a mysterious intruder.

They must be visitors from another world disguised as dreams.

No better way to stay in tune with one's fear of tornados.

He was turning me into a bas-relief on the sofa —  I was starting
to feel like upholstery —

I looked over his shoulder and saw another guy stride across the
room and vanish into the kitchen — The front door was locked.

Soon we are all gone like our instinct for what is and isn't edible.


17.
He's the surest kind of hypocrite — an atheist who insists God
alone can judge.

We are all leaving the table like the disciples in da Vinci's *Last
Supper* — not one by one — not in amorous couples.

We leave the centerpiece on its own — here and in the Garden.

His face, like his doctrine, becomes more and more nebulous.

Was tempera a mistake or an exodus?

18.
My Waterpik, upright in its holster — the toothbrush on its
charger — a white Brancusi — I need more allies like these.

People from all over the world sing, "It's fun to stay at the
YMCA!" stretching themselves into unwitting semaphores.

They flourish their unwitting support across the mud like Raleigh's
cape — scratch it in the sand and dare themselves to cross it —
tee it up like a golf ball or a skull and invite themselves to kick it.

19.
In a lecture hall the professor teaches us a German song full of
snow and bonfires and a mother and a child.

We swell like a choir thrilled with itself till the professor whispers,
"Good work — You've just sung a Nazi hymn" — An accordion
hung from the cross's shoulders.

20.
Sometimes it's not interesting — It's an old photo from which
every detail has faded.

Or it's counterproductive — a rotary fan spun by heat from a
flame.

It's a shameful cure for shame. You lay it at your father's feet, a
grab bag of recriminations.

You pour a circle of salt around your father's tomb as though he
were a margarita.

The recriminations gather outside your father's door like carolers.


21.
We blaze so long as we have flesh to burn — He's hiding inside us where we'll never look.

He wraps his meat in butcher's paper knowing that's the meat we'll never cook.

They cut off my stick, laid it at his feet, dared him to pick it up.

He smiled and said, "If you doubt my hypocrisy, remember the composers' sins don't dampen my love for their symphonies.

If you doubt my hunger, check your vital organs."


22.
The dervishes' skirts are laser sharp.

Just as you eventually beg the best lover to stop, you wind up cursing the djinn.

I'm tired and bored — Even my excitement is yawning.

Dervishes and dreidels and rotary fans — some inspired by flame, some by electric current — beg me to stop their spinning.

The last two years of high school I lived in notebooks — sometimes writing, sometimes igniting — uselessly feeling the difference between the two.

23.

Ellen changed her name to Nancy — Raymond, the youngest, alone survives.

Nannie remembered, when she sat on his lap, her father suffered her to play with his pocket watch as though it were a bird.

His temper and his other family he kept in the other pocket.

Ellen/Nancy saw what Nannie couldn't see — Raymond was born with a clubfoot.

Mom was in the bathroom arguing with her makeup — In the living room Nancy and Nannie discussed Anita Hill's testimony — Nancy defined oral sex for her sister.

Mom says it's the most surreal conversation that has ever occurred in the annals of sisterhood.

He spent his first year with a doctor — His foot was partially cured.

Because he was born younger than they, because he limped, because he didn't know his own family, his sisters babied him.

His first wife waited on him — His second told him to get off the sofa and square dance.

They square danced all the way to Micronesia, where they were treated like gods and fed delicacies that made them sick.

24.

From dizzy windows mothers drop their children through the smoke closing around them.

They hear the firemen's voices — They don't see their faces.

God plants madness in our dreams as a warning of what lies ahead if we continue to pursue him.

Tracked by grace, hounded by miracles, we resist the fiat as long as we can.

When the firemen look up, something like a sluice pours noisily from the backs of their helmets.


25.

Throughout the cinematic night I hear a man whistling at regular intervals.

His air is both comforting and ominous like Robert Mitchum singing "Leaning on the Everlasting Arm" in *The Night of the Hunter.*

Thinking of Charles Laughton as fat Henry VIII and Quasimodo, I'm saddened by his dreams of blokes he knew in the cyclist battalion with bikes slenderer, lighter, quieter, more obedient than stallions.

LOVE and HATE on Robert Mitchum's knuckles flare in my face as he punches.

He masturbated with only one of these hands — He would use both on his penitentiary rivals and lovers.

26.
A man in a wheelchair is stranded in the men's room at a rest stop.

Everything must be relearned — how to whisper a word in one's own ear.

Art cannot survive ultimate resolution — The artist can't survive unending suspension.

It was so much work to get here, he's in no hurry to leave.


27.
Outside — an ice cream truck's glockenspiel — a lonely voice calling someone who's not there — an angry voice shouting at someone who's not there.

Inside — accidental sounds of two people trying to out-wait each other — The ambulatory one's unlikely to be the more patient.

The parting of the Red Sea — an imposition of unsustainable order — A Venus flytrap teaches the waters to close.

Be polite — Wait for pauses in your own speech.

The paraplegic might be waiting as Jesus waited for the Roman's spear.

Satiety and hunger — indistinguishable for those who can't tell past from future.


28.
He wrote *The Children's Crusade* in a day, slumped in a stall smaller than Bunyan's or Cleaver's cell.

Vergil claps one hand over Dante's eyes and pushes with the other.

Thighs chilled by marble, he joins Pygmalion and swears to stop salting himself.

He wrote the crusade one child at a time — groups of five lying end to end, stretching to the horizon like hope and hopelessness.

There were three kinds of kid — those who screamed when stepped on — those who were silent and those who sang.


29.
Where are the hands that circumcised me? Were they gentle or merely expert? Did they perfect other acts few of us attempt?

Did they ever strike the taut membrane of the conga or the tom-tom?

Transgender citizens are outnumbered — Like the por — like all tax brackets — they are always with us.

They are like drums in their antiquity and ubiquity — They are not like drums insofar as, not all Peoples beat upon them.

He was as good a cook as he was a mohel. The tiny penis heads pretended to be strawberries. The strawberries believed they were good-sized penis heads.

The mohel/chef never noticed his own confusion.

30.

Northern California Cherry Blossom Festival — San Francisco
Taiko Dojo.

Both heads of the awesome drum are under attack — Each
drummer bending far, far back, the way I used to pull my thumb
to my wrist to prove to other first graders I was double-jointed.

And this is but a speck compared to the three-ton o-daiko cut
from a thousand-year-old tree, immovable in its temple.

Even the women drummers turn me on — The Goddess of the
Sun, who, withdrawing into a cave, darkens the world.

The goddess Ame No Uzume, whose  lascivious stomping on a
wooden tub, the first taiko drum, entices light to return.

Let one of the drummers be the color of bark — Let one be
perfectly erect, a young tree — Let there be sunbaked hippies
with biblical beards and biblical hippies with sunbaked beards.

The sand of Nokomis beach is like asphalt — The drummers
have paunches, ball caps and T shirts — Their sunglasses give
them the expressionless faces of insects.

Their lawn chairs are a species of basket.

Ame No Uzume dances with a Hula-Hoop and a veil of lamé —
May the hands that carved these drums carve me.

31.

Joy you're born with is no good if you don't know how to use it.

Naturalized citizens of the Republic of Joy are eligible for the
presidency.

Every night he goes to bed imagining the perfect stick.

Every morning we go out together and hunt for it.

If I were rich, I'd spend heaven and earth to obtain one of those early Roman depictions of Jesus, a curly-headed youth in a toga with a wand.


32.
Gregg and Suzanne were studying for a Russian exam — We kept the line open all night.

From toke to toke, they held the receiver between them and listened to my sleep — my breathing, which was as close as they could come.

Companions fall from the sky — meteorites and redwings in Arkansas and Winnipeg.

We live near the station — The train is slowing — With its lights on at night we read the faces of riders stirring to disembark.

Why am I now joyful — Why am I not joyful — which is the typo? — I chant.


33.
I did it — got my hair cut short enough for me to wear a saffron robe and live from a begging bowl.

First I thought it looked shameful and was glad — a needed blow to vanity — Later I decided it looked pretty good.

Saul gets knocked from his horse — sees the light, but not all of it — becomes Paul — does not become that which is not named.

Becomes Paul, whom John blamed and Yoko, whom Paul held responsible.

When I put the airplane window to sleep, my senses can't tell if I'm seven miles above the earth or seven miles below it or being digested in the guts of a deafening machine.

Ugolino is a little less hungry than he was before — As for Icarus, the sky's as hostile as the sea.

The artists, some of whom care for the drowned litheness while others care for their reputations, conspire to console Daedalus.

We feel so mature when we get our first clock-radio and start waking up before our parents to solve Ellery Queen mysteries, wash and feed ourselves for school.

Walk — Leave your virgin sheets — The boy who lay beside you is now a deadbeat dad.

Under what straw should I plant these engraved plates? "I seek no victory for the honor of my soul" (Maimonides).

My pizza cutter reflects more of my face than your knife reflects of yours. Paul, but never wholly Paul.


34.
"I seek a soul for my dishonor's victory" (Me)

He's not cutting grass — The grass is already lower than the blade — He's just drowning out his thoughts.

Mike talks of the boat people and a cousin raped by pirates and trouble in Orange County.

A Vietnamese merchant has hung the Communist flag outside his shop — a glutton for meaning.

The only other way out was through Cambodia.


35.
I cultivate my fear of heights by staying as low as I can — pull Whitman's beard — see if he's really Santa Claus, the shaman sliding down the chimney, down the tree — Spin Sartre's eye like a top.

Images flee into dreams — Oh it's bright there — lit by a thousand sins — blinded by a thousand pardons.

There's a voice within each voice — Poppers help me feel elephants swimming in infinity.

An Asian man in a tailored suit is walking around United Nations Plaza, waving a sign that reads:

IMPEACH CLINTON, ROOSEVELT, JEFFERSON AND WASHINGTON.

The only way out is through the Muni station.

36.
He sits on a milk crate trimming his beard — The scissors are real — The mirror is not.

The Aztecs were right — The Spaniards and their horses were a single beast.

This cabbie used to be a dentist — He couldn't go on filling his patients' teeth with mercury-tainted amalgam.

Is he to be believed?

Some nights, exhaust from buses pulling out is the only warmth he feels.

If I'd met the Centaur Cortez, what cocktail of fear and rejoicing would I have offered — would I have drunk?

I relish this headline: AIDS monkeys freed by Hurricane Andrew — The lab says none of the monkeys were infected — I said the same about myself.


37.
"NATO don't care who they blow up," says the sage of Tina's Cafe, his newspaper spread generously on the counter.

What will ensue when the escaped AIDS monkeys catch up with the Children's Crusade — become the head or the tail — march two by two — have a contest to see who chews best?

"You can't tutor that girl anymore — can't be alone in the house with her — Something goes wrong, they blame you" — So says my fiancé's mom.

His family's from Hanoi — The girl's is from Saigon.

Both in southern California now — Maybe someday they'll
actually leave Vietnam — which by then may be gone and will
certainly have re-dawned beyond recognition.


38.
A lawn chair, a folding table for my laptop — in the quiet garage
I'd be lonesome without the susurrant traffic.

My shadow doesn't fit on the page — He held his flesh captive
— eternity, his demand.

Good rough flowers — an apt subject for a woodcut if I could
cut wood.

He has more magic than he has good sense — and no origins yet.


39.
In the public health clinic — a man slumps like a tall bag of rice
— He's broken by three days of hiccuping.

Silence wants us to have voice and music and MRI machines.

Silence is not a jealous lover — That's why we always go back to her.

Listening to John Tavener's "Thunder Enters Her" — I lie naked
on the striped green sheets — just blessed by a young Mandarin
born in Arkansas, raised in Tennessee — He sounded like Clinton
as he pulled on his jeans.

40.

On my 16th Ken gave me a get well soon card — crossed out *well* and wrote in *some.*

The same friend who, thanks to an Exacto knife, gave me a sign that read BEWARE OF GOD (not dog) (which I thought was the meaning of my name).

Now 33 years and scores of guys later I can almost say I've had enough.


41.

Gatorade and Stouffer's meatballs for lunch — monthly inspection by a Filipino with the 'pen' name Nathan.

Possibly he read the label on my mailbox and knows I gave him my legal name — Maybe he understands I did this to ensure I feel a tremor when he says Tim.

It's not just lean — It's cuisine.

A bout with IBS — churning that Jesus couldn't have calmed — Appetite returns — Mizue's cooking Nabe.

I tell Satoru (her husband) I can't see "Tomb Raider" with them — My boyfriend's coming to town and I want to be with him.

"Yes, yes," he says, "you have to be with him."


42.

He's no longer bridled by personality — It's not important that this is liberating.

New air is as likely to blow foul as it is to blow fair.

Rough trade is out of bounds — A good sized fly could knock him down.

Two long notes from a car horn — could be the signal to unleash a new hound — could be all that's left of impatient *Taps*.

There's no denying word leads to word — hopefully unexpected — like *trampoline* — then to unsuspected couplings, *a demon trampoline*.


43.
I can't read the message he left on the back of my throat — or his teethmarks in the rim of a styrofoam cup.

I'm reminded how he liked to say for most the Pacific Rim was a region — For him it was a vocation.

This is what it must sound like in the head of a fish cast upon the shore — a man with no openings longing to be intoxicated — a man with too many openings longing to be drunk.


44.
The universe has granted me permission to give you all of this —

And though it's only a fraction of all I am, it's enough to keep me giving.

Stars call to each other like whales and my only regret is all those inseams I pressed my mouth to could have been mouths of the electrocuted, the half-drowned, the cardiac-arrested.


45.
If you lift this burden from me again, I doubt if I'll survive the
relief.

I like to think of that glass pipe — not much longer than a pinky
— swallowed and crushed by a garbage truck —

shattering like a personality designed for lesser responsibilities —
the sound of its breaking lost in hydraulic grinding.

I think of the shape it gave the smoke — and the mutations that
would change it to a brain.


46.
Man does not live by poison alone — I needed to say that like I
need another hole in my forehead.

There's nothing inspiring about the idea of books that can only be
read when they're burning.

For an instant I think I'm writing in the dark — Then I realize my
eyes are glowing.

Even if Allah dictated these sticks, my name would not last forever.


47.
Video cassettes and empty cardboard sheaths clutter the floor —
He and the screen try to stare each other down.

12:39 — The ramen block is softening — Writing those great poems that drove him away — I'm as unemployable as sperm in the belly.

*Le drumstick de mon frère* — a commemorative 7-up bottle — three fingers of Vaseline — Swing Low Sweet Solitude — Solicitude.


48.
Wind keeps Mother and flags awake — The waves keep talking — Many directives are intelligible!

I close my eyes and count the anonymous — How wrong I was, thinking they entered my stable to deposit their Wise Men's gifts.

More than three of the Wise Men were actually coal miners.

The way he undressed a stick of gum — oblivious — broke my heart.

49.
Beware of hookups who claim to be tops but start whittling the candles as soon as you leave the room — of therapists who look down on shamans — of ministers and zoo keepers who've forgotten what beasts the gods are — of people who claim there's such a thing as artificial darkness — of neurologists who claim that remembering our dreams is akin to the theft of fire — of poets who don't fear words.


50.
Also he who sits upon thy face, pivots upon thy tongue, but does not thank thee for the instant oatmeal or the warm dry bedding or

the quiet answers to his questions.

Suddenly I'm standing face-to-face with my self-righteousness
— I stick my tongue out at it and it sticks it back out at me.


51.
Some say God's only comfort is that the dead don't evolve —

But then I hear the silence of a bush that will not burn —

I see the seed, cast upon a blazing rock, bear fruit — rock candy.

Someone dropped hot wax on my throat — Unlike Psyche, he
didn't do it by accident.

A Muslim student has one foot on the floor, one in the sink — He
balances like an egret so evolved, so refined.


52.
My grandmother said to me, "I seen pigeons flyin' low, and I
seen people flyin' even lower."

Mona doesn't pay much attention to the obsessive-compulsive
man at Denny's in his T-shirt and scout-master pants, rocking —
flipping the flaps of the little jukebox on the wall.

Some days there's random violence — like a Bible falling open to
certain passages — Other days there's a fierce debate among
the gentle instincts.

I applaud his vast repertory of tics and wonder what triggers them —

a vision of himself being cut from the womb, crying, "This is not
the entrance promised in the script!"


53.
I punish myself for your birthday — abrading my cheeks on his
unshaven chin.

I'm as pointless as the prophet of a repentant people — I know
all about the treasure that rusts in heaven — There's no more
*panis agelicus* in the breadbox.

Dogs sing atop the grass — then hurl themselves past Aztecs
quietly peddling weed —


past foreign clerics who wonder, "We'd what — we'd better or
we'd better not?"


54.
He had black fingernails — His astrological necklace swung
back and forth an inch from my chest — a straight line indicating
my heart would bear a boy-child.

Mom and I know she started drinking coffee again — despite her
oncologist's counsel.

Dad and I know my friends and I were naked in the swimming
pool at our graduation party.

My partner and I know why I owed so much to the Bank of
America.

Everyone except Toni knows she was adopted — Most of us know what the police found in Sarah's trunk — We feign ignorance to spare her mother.


55.
A dog licked away Saint Rock's infection as though it were the salt in his sweat.

"It's a wonderful story — that any creature — saint, dog or ape — should make kindness a habit."

This book is the best actor alive — That actor's the best living book.

One, two, three — lift together — One, two, three, live together — One, two, three, leave together.


56.
I lift the hair over his nape and startle the lizard there — It freezes in self-defense.

Something speaks through me — I accept never knowing what it is — no misplaced pride — no liability.

It's wrong to compare him to the Eucharist — He needs no transubstantiation.

He'll infect anyone, clergy or laity.


57.
In the Sufaibo his chopsticks linger above a tofu cube on my plate.

When his belly is opened white liquid oozes out — a thousand nights' half-digested pearls.

Look, the first birds have eaten only half of the moon — surfeited? or kindly leaving plenty for us?

58.
Eyes all around, fixed on the screen — I palpate the underside of his thighs.

He holds his bag on his lap as though he's awaiting the boarding announcement — waiting for his zone to be called.

59.
We're too late to see the bird take flight — The twig like a diving board regains its composure.

Apparently waiting for the Messiah is like waiting for a pot to boil — Keep your eyes on the pot.

If you miss one bus, you can always attract the next one — In the city, the wait's not long.

60.
He had three tongue-studs — They felt like ball bearings in a perfect machine.

A middle-aged Russian held the elevator gate — Taylor Street — The only neighbor I spoke to more than once.

Immigrant from a country where strangers converse — he was finding out this is not one of those countries — Unfortunately it was nothing personal.

The cage rocked as though he were shaking it with his fists — We were standing as still as we could, the stillest we would stand for days.


61.
A hummingbird sounds like a Geiger counter flitting around Chernobyl.

I wish I knew how to say, "Don't close your eyes," in Thai.

My advice to the eyes: diversify — Don't remove the specks — Let them multiply.

In September 1997 my vocabulary was incomplete — no raw breeding, no tweaking, no Atripla, no trolling, no Obamacare — *Fraught* was still *fraught with something* — set adrift — like our words.


62.
The mountains are wedded to one another — a parade of polygamy stretching farther than the eye can see.

Calling and calling to Flandrin's "Jeune homme nu assis au bord de la mer"— knowing he'll never lift or even turn his head from his knees is reason enough to go on calling.

63.

After the clubs I see a hummingbird walking in the bare street.
I tell my sister-in-law — That's how I learn she thinks
hummingbirds have no feet.

What say you, Yusuf Islam? It pleased me when I was ten — It
still pleases me — flames in black and white films.


64.

A cop in Vicco Kentucky speaking of the Mayor — "Yeah I
know he's gay, and yeah he's my best friend — That boy knows
more about me than most people in my life — and I love him like
a brother, and I'll take care of him just like that, just like a
brother."

Instrument 1 — a feeder that sighs when a hummingbird licks
sugar water from its tube — hunter and prey in collusion —
strangers meeting by chance at the edge of a cliff — joining
hands — stepping into the abyss.

Instrument 2 — a chain-link fence being climbed — falling into
the updraft of his arms — vanishing like a single whispered
command — sliding into the passenger seat of his van.

Instrument 3 — a leaf-blower — Instrument 4 — kids romping
through leaves not driven away by instrument 3.


65.

Wait till you have a range of purple sticks — start the sticks'
cloud house.

When I took up the hexagrams, I found skewers made fine,
pointy, sharp substitutes for yarrow.

# Pandemic Year

My Spring class was a standup that
lacked the chutzpa to shame, shut up
or survive the viral heckler shouting
insults from a cornered table, a dark
party made even darker by the spot-

light attacking my face. No Summer,
Autumn or new Spring terms for me.
Without trying, I learned to neglect,
royally, my school email account for
days. I began dreaming my pajamas

and thighs were wedded like a burn
victim's polyester and flesh. Who,
anymore, aspires to such weddings?
Lacking weekends, the year became
a year only in the academic sense.

Lacking real sense, plunges into the
extravagant side of simile couldn't
have been avoided. Weeks made of
productive sabbaths? The shutdown
was too short for those to flourish.

Through that unholy year I gathered
money from the air, spent it on daily
dares, held my breath both literally
and communally, and relearned the
old, hard way of estimating deaths.

# Address Stickers

They were kin to Easter
Seals. The National Wild-
life Federation tucked
them into appeals for do-
nations. On some, Mike's
name squatted sure on our
address. On all the rest,

mine sat like roosters on
nests, strangely not out
of place. I used them all.
Some were feelers to old
lovers forsaken at flood's
first breath. They flew
back with Noah's first

birds. Others managed to
be the beaks that didn't
return. Unlike Noah, I
wondered if they were
unlucky spies eaten by
crocs with hard snouts.
I used some to track down

girls who had crushes on
me, whom I disappointed
(I longed for their brothers).
I wanted to know if at last
they understood the kind-

ness I'd done them and
the maturity I possessed at

fifteen that some fellow
gays are still searching for.
One went to the mailman
with a broad accent and
wingspan; one to Naomi at
Sherwin hyphen Williams;
one to the grandmother

who thought I'd want a girl
if I changed my pallor to a
farmer's tan. Many went
to isolationist seas made to
admit they are one water.
Many, in questionnaires,
asked lands to clarify if

they liked the wet storm
or preferred to stay dry.
It was an era of too much
screen time. I had to use
the seals before carriers
were quarantined and
mail became a crime.

# Uplift

Not every sun can be the Elephant
Sun that pushes not just night but
also the darkness of the mind from

the sky. When Elephant Sun rears,
swing your trunk, such as it is, in an
elegant question mark and trumpet

with your longest breath, the one
you've been saving up. And when
ES goes, backing up like a butler,

don't bow or turn your head. Look
honestly at the horizon — or at
the skyline if that's all you've got.

# All Your Life

What adjective/verb fits truthfully into
a question ending with *all your life*?
*Alive* or a brother verb? *Breathing*?

The air above us is untouched and pale.
The grass is trodden pale. Cattle, bulky
and graceful, walked here long ago and

lately. They are walking here now,
pulling and barking their kids more or
less into place. They hold bratwursts,

burritos and ice cream to their mouths.
I can't help thinking of harmonicas and
microphones. For you and me it's dogs

you swear are buttered. The Visitor's
Center calls the gathering: A Taste of
Kenosha. Annual, it's on the same shore

(cooled, even chilled by an ancient lake)
as the Pride and Labor and Memorial
and Independence festivals. Our first

year here we expected the city's most
modern ristoranti, bistros, fusion cafés
with entrees on billowing table cloths.

Now, knowing better or worse, we stroll
resigned as steers, licking butter or lard
on our lips. We pass the pendulum pirate

ship (mockery of progress fraught with
excited screams); dogs of all extremes
that don't know they're competing to see

how far into a pool they can leap; bands
whose talent or lack of talent is blunted
by big bad speakers. We pass another

male couple on the walking side of the
foot/bike path. The tall one says, "Why
have you been [garbled] all your life?"

# Amazon

2:33 a.m.. My Amazon
order has shipped. What
do you know, I'm really
getting "The Little
Foxes" DVD next day,

delivered free. Herbert
Marshall will announce
to Bette Davis, "The
problem with this damn
rain is, it comes from

gray clouds of blame."
Davis will counter,
"That is why it is good.
Its damage and its aid
will not be the random

damage and aid of our
ordinary rain." In the
shower I ask myself:
What's the very hottest
rain that ever fell on us?

That ever will fall?
What would water as
hot as this pleasing
shower do to stability?
Enjoying my shave,

I remember a guy I
showered with once.
As I lathered his back,
his almost drowned
voice spoke of his

Sleeping Beauty fear
of razors — how it
made him careful
and careless of both
chores and pleasures —

and of showers with his
Dad before and after
the public pool; of the
ladies' room with Mom
when he was still

very small; glad Dad
was not as naive as
Marshall; Mom not as
cruel, petty and blind-
sided as the great Bette.

# Prehistoric Survivor

When I went to get my flu shot
and the lovely brown medallion
it placed on my right shoulder
which hurt when I forgot and

rolled on it in my sleep — when
I tried a walk-in and the new
receptionist told me the doctor's
schedule, which I thought as

immutable as the order of the
seasons, had changed — when
I went to pick up my meds 30
minutes early and wandered

around that neighborhood where
houses grow up from seeds
watered by cold, dirty rain, as
unwanted, as un-genocide-able

as weeds — I came upon what
looked like a pair of enormous
willow trees fused into a swaying
green dinosaur, heading for the

hovel of a hoarder whose hoard
had spilled out into his yard —
no it was too orderly to have
spilled. If I were a video artist

I would make a feature length
video — one long tracking shot
moving meticulously over the
limbs of this piecemeal gallery.

Translucent blue bags bulging
with clouds of Kleenex typing
paper. Lifeless Duracells and
Energizers, brave leaden infantry.

Sheets of pegboard softening
in the rain like the brown parts
of ice cream sandwiches. Dolls
with Jim Bean feeling no pain.

Embodiments of uncalled for
certainties, paths crooked and
straight simultaneously, simple
notions no human can explain.

And over all this, the double
tree, paralyzed in its stride.

# Ghost of the Rose

Act I, before the big curtain
goes up, is the most intricate,
intimate, subtle. No one takes
it all in. Critics ignore it. The

warning of the house, when
the crowd prepares to believe
in spirit achievements of the
flesh, is also an item unto itself.

Then, one by one, like glass
dominos tipping each other
over, the spectators feel the
impossibility of these feats.

They shudder or whistle with
relief, knowing Eros, afraid of
being caught, will never kiss
Psyche again. This has nothing

to do with me. The orchestra
sweeps it all under the apron
and the rose appears in tights
with codpiece and a mind that

bulge as though they too were
muscles. The final act is set
in the lobby, in taxis, in bed-
rooms, where modern theater

goers surmise that, among
the first spectators, only the
appalled admitted the show
was as warm as a good review.

# The Ghost of the Rose

(for Vaslav Nijinsky)

Collaborators that never meet. That
require interpreters. That are tossed
with the programs. A few still shine.
Diaghilev, Nijinsky, Weber. One, in
a rush, falls through a trapdoor. His

rings leap and run not very far, then
relax unharmed on a concrete floor.
I cast myself as the debutante in a
wet gown, folds acrid from waltzing,
arches aching, stomach growling —

too late to wake my maid. In the red
lobby, whiskey sour in hand, bored
by well prepared accolades, all I feel
is the closeness of my coat and the
dark that will walk with me arm in

arm, gossiping about the costume
rushed in on the very last train, silk
petals torn and askew, the set-maker
kneeling in place of the costumier,
Vaslav wincing, cursing in Russian

as pins through the tricot prick his
skin; cursing the man tuxedoed and
top-hatted, whose voice could not

be resisted at the Hotel Europa; who
made Vaslav "tremble like a leaf"

when they made love the moment
they met. "Talk again about the stage
hands who night after night catch
him in warm white towels. Tell me
about the servant gathering petals

from the boards and the costume
mistress backstage when the stars
go drinking and screwing." "With
curling iron, bony hands and skill,
she calms and reshapes wilted silk."

# Heatwave

Night is Heatwave's trick.
If we weren't receptive,
we wouldn't know we

need teasing. The living
room hoards every breath
of conditioned air. There's

a numbness about the
limbs and an altered state
of wind. We think we're

about to sleep, but that's
more teasing. A chill has
seized your internal organs.

I can't grasp why your
breath is not the coolant
that would stop our gasping

as the decrepit luxury
appliance can't — though
it is endowed with

cussedness that stops the
airlessness from stifling
us. On the floor you realize

your belt can be a rope
with which we can lasso
ice sculptures. On the

floor on our bellies or
backs there's no danger
we'll slip and rip our

slacks. Sleep creeps to us
like a soldier on tired,
tense, sweaty elbows.

# Take Up Your Bed

Sometimes I joke with the other tired beggars,
"This primitive street's not my bed. My ear to
the ground listens for stampede, for Colonel

Custer, for rescuing Indians." As we are barely
in the Christian era, my fellow mendicants
don't get the references — why Indians? —

for me this is the joke. This morning I heard
a sandal-step I knew well. When it stopped,
I opened my eyes to feet that will pace in

Heaven after strolling through Hell. Or so they
intimate. Dusty and hard, far from appetizing,
in need of ointment no beggar can afford, they

stood there flexing their toes. Before he could say
what I knew he would say, not raising my head
I suggested he lie beside me and relax. A brief

pause. A brief laugh. He stroked my head, then
went on his way. "Someday," I thought. "Some-
day for sure. He can't skirt dirt beds forever."

# April 6, 2020

Today it's generic raisins and the
one allowed scroll of primitive TP.
Mike does all the shopping. My
superior years and shy T cells
make me his stand-in sacred bull.

Summer 2019 I timed my walks
around our Aldi-CVS parking
lot to opening hours, most days
powered by croissants (too-cheap-
to-be-good pleasures) to remind

Mike of the toasty advantages of
marrying an early-riser. Maybe
we were low on milk ("$1.39
in Wisconsin — $4.00 in L.A."
he bragged to his mother.) May-

be I wanted to greet the friendly
woman behind the counter who
knew my head was a radio and
wanted to sample the record spin-
ning at that old-school station.

Maybe it was, "I'm just a soul
whose intentions are good." Or
"On the bloody morning after,
one tin soldier rides away." This
year my window sees shoppers

with red bandanas covering their
breath, trundling the risky haul
to their trunks. Imagine explorers
returning from space, thinking
mobs of Jesse James wannabes

now loot the supermarkets. They
open late, close earlier and earlier.
I wait until nine and walk for 20
heart-healthy minutes. I re-create
visions of a monk who survived

the new Black Death orbiting his
monastery where evening birds
sing nothing to do with Vespers.
Mike, who has never been much
of a window gazer, has acquired

an unnerving custom. I don't ask.
Still, I know he is monitoring the
lot's auto population with worry.
What will it mean when it's bare
as a bankrupt car dealership, or

when there are a dozen, as it was
before this started? Inserting a
finger between two blinds, is he
the Doubting Thomas trembling
at the last certainty? Gazing out,

is he Noah, whose vigil yearns to
subside with the mind-drowning
damp? Fathom by fathom, I revert

to my childhood faith, to others'
pre-fab prayers air knows well.

Is prayer no better than, and as
harmful as injecting our veins
with bleach? Are we missing
the symbolism this whitening
substance tries so hard to teach?

Picture a literally white world.
Bleached sky and earth. All sands,
mountains, running and resting
and dead water blanched. The
wide White Death entrenched.

# Archetypes

My first boyfriend tells me to stop looking
for archetypes. My second, going further,
says, "Avoid them altogether. If you see

one coming, cross the street. Duck into the
Five and Dime." "Why do you say Five
and Dime?" I ask  (curious, concerned,

irritated). "I don't know," he replies
(defensive? wondering? not really paying
attention to his own thoughts?). Later when

he is plumping up his pillows in that way
of his, he says, "I guess it's cause my Dad
mentioned a Five and Dime on the square

and wondered if I remembered it at all, and
if I did, did I recall the smell of the little red
peanuts they roasted all day — a bag big

enough for any two hungry boys — for just
five cents." I hope this will be my last boy-
friend. The trajectory of this vignette implies

a third would urge me to slay any archetype
that crosses my path — a slaughter that
would leave us utterly atypical and pathless.

# One Who Will Not Hear

Peter to Mary Magdalen. "Remember
when He was in a rotten mood, like
Norman Mailer with writer's block
and we came upon a man as sturdy as
a platoon…" "And the man cried,

'Hosannah!' and the teacher cried,
'Your faith has made you sick,' and on
the spot the troop became a crumbling
garden of lepers." "Remember how
upset we all were? Well, I was thrilled."

My analyst to me: "Why do you keep
repeating *Arrow, Arrow*?" Me: "No,
I said, 'Narrow, Narrow is the road.'"
"I swear on a stack of burning Bibles
you said, 'Arrow, arrow is the code.'"

# Ashes and Other Packing Materials

"I don't know how much milk it takes.
Don't try the casserole yet." She was

sitting among 55 boxed-up years, ready
to abandon the longest stretch of their/our

lives, three days from trading false
security for the final brief adventure.

Can you blame me for thinking of
Pompeii? I can. Can you explain

why I'm thinking of Pompeii? I can't.
Let us go out today — or this weekend

at the latest — looking for lost items that
don't make sense. Let us be the highest

or the lowest point in a landscape.
Let us not be picky about the terrain.

Those who are picky, find themselves
empty as unclaimed moving pods

that will squat on the lot till the city gods
won't put off the blacktopping any longer.

# The Improbable Dream

At last a peace-held moment. No
roofing crews in high gear or
warring MRI magnets. Virtual
fires on plasma screens play kind
tricks on chilly minds and skins.

No Canadian fires launch the un-
thinkable: a Canadian attack, be
it only smoke, on a United States
that launches nothing, not even
drones. No one eaten up about

their job. No money-medicine
collisions. No Cain killing an
Abel pursuant to their maker's
poor parenting skills. One mind-
boggling host of angels halts the

down strokes of uncountable
Abrahams of every kind, while
another host gently binds the
mouth that uttered the command,
and no one is made in the image

of a singer or Lord who, happy,
dashes little ones on the rocks.
At last. At last. But how long
is a moment? It's impossible to
measure when one is asleep.

# Bedroom Scene

He rises into sleep. I gather
his forearm crutches from
the corner where they rest.
My mind is still and I come
away empty-handed as if

the stillness has placed the
crutches beyond any theft's
reach. A phrase tugs at my
boxer briefs. Is this how
he feels when he's alone?

Say, pole fishing or bathing
when sex and paraplegia
are less than glints on the
horizon? Does he think in
the boat: This is how Tim

feels when he's not listening
to me; reading or ogling.
Air blunders into my face
like a bug. Fifty decisions
line up, a tense firing squad.

Fifty await their turn with
the blindfold. I see shade
and the mountains it implies.
I hear a silence say what
no other silence ever did.

I see crutches that clack in
my hands like cranes — as
plain, as used (like grocery
bags) as dark and shocking
as swords about to cross.

# Bedtime Story

I sleep with my laptop under my pillow.
I wake feeling broody with laptop hair.
I sleep clamped to your leg like a car
boot. I wake cramped on your leg like a

dog. Three mornings a week, last-night
rice gets fried and offered. Once a
week I accept. Good as sun's gold
in my eyes were raisins I added today, to

your brief surprise and disapproving
amusement. I sleep with my head on a
stone where pole, tree, totem or goal-
post part the soil. My clothes convert

like Elizabeth Taylor to something old
and Middle Eastern. The angels —
or aliens? — jogging on that ramp —
it's a wonder they don't trample me.

# Yellow

Three months after the hospital's elevators,
cut big for wheelchairs, made me feel like
lost freight; after I made the very common

mistake of thinking nurses my friends;
after I watched Mike, who rescued my
height, shrink to fit a makeshift, two-chair

cot in the corner of a private sick room,
the April and May that promised to be my
last broke their word. Their birds, turning

canary, hopped to the window, parted
the curtains with their beaks, flew and laid
wings on my un-burning cheeks. Buds, even

the greenest, were as yellow as his expression
and tired eyes. I would learn how to live and
thrive knowing I had caused that fatigue.

He would learn, in spite of occasional
resentment, to see the colors we applied to
each other as proof of our tightening league.

# A Young Man's Tale

There were a few (I'd say five)
Summers that failed to sear and
Winters that barely froze. I was
Piaf and Brel. Pre-Colombian
meant Billie Holiday on Deko,

pre-John Hammond. Then one
day I found online effigies of
those Peruvian dudes. Vessels
waiting to be filled, not actually
waiting at all. Kiln-baked mates

in earthenware love, uninfected
by Church, congratulating each
other on their nature in keenly
penetrating fashions. Manuels
and Jorges were close behind.

Acquaintances with tales that
begged me to dig into history.
Then came Miguel. Anyplace
he or I had a key to, we turned
into an Andean summit driven

clean by savage winds. Then
came shame. No, not  the one
you're imagining. But shame
for what one country does to
another country it calls friend.

# Death of a Car

I wreck the car to prove
you love me as Aquinas
proves God is a fool and
that means God must be
real. Unless it proves that

Thom is the fool, which
leaves God as the penny
toss he has always been.
I wreck the car as I loll
on the floor in blankets

my sleep always messes
up. Water is in my eyes
once more — no, it is on
my eyes as it is on Earth,
everywhere the premise

of all surmise that shows
itself worth only half its
worth. I kill the car to
prove I love you down to
your anger, which I hate.

# Camille

If there's any chance of imagining
yourself as Jacob Camille Pissarro
at 25, try. If there's a chance small

as a brush stroke to feel your body
as the shapely bristles of a perfect
new paintbrush, please try. Even if

it's as brief as a flash of white sail
in the air or on a taut canvas, use
all you are given. Use all you steal.

# Ghost Facts

What few people know about
ghosts: They don't talk, they
bark. Many times, when I'm

up in the dark getting ready
to travel or being pestered by
an idea, I hear woofing on

the other side of seeing (i.e.
the alley) and think: Sally
Gomez sure is walking that

poor dog early. Uh-uh. That
is neither Sally nor her mutt.
It is the ghost of John Lennon

that tried to float a feather
from room to room in his
and Yoko's Dakota flat. He

missed by an iota and now
the plume that could scratch
lyrics in the Beyond floats

around our apartment. Mike
takes it for a preview of my
otherworld return to this hut.

# Not to Mention his Ruddy Cheeks

Briefly Nijinsky danced for me,
raved and filled my notebooks
with red eyes.
Not from crying.
Not from drug or drink.
Not from being rubbed mercilessly
against a man's thighs. A searching,
unfriendly energy
sparked those fires as a flashlight
beam reddens a fox's pupils.
Vaslav didn't push his brother.
It didn't enter his mind till after
his brother fell;
after the little doctor came
and pronounced his brother
irremediably ill;
after his mother, unable to
pay the little doctor's big bill,
gave his brother to the state
as though he were a tax
mercifully payable in flesh.
And what if he had pushed?
Hadn't birth thrust him
into a shoving world?
Didn't his father pitch all
three kids into a pond
before they knew that what
the fish in their brains were
attempting was called

surviving? Didn't his teachers push
him painfully up on his toes
as though there were a garden wall
and an orchard to peek into?
Didn't Diaghilev push him
to his knees the second
the bellboy was dismissed? Were
his leaps that humbled
the history of dance
rebounds from that genuflection?

# Crêpe Myrtle

1.
Magnus: Look what I brought you from the antipodes.
The New World will call it Crêpe Myrtle.
Carl: The train is coming. How about that boxcar?
Magnus: Across the Great Plains we will hurtle.


2.
Who complains as generously as I do? Who wears
dishonor like me? What questions stand starker
against stumps, sunups and downs —
famous tourist attractions?

My genus name is cooler than yours.
Lagerstroemia. Touch it and shiver.

My namesake, Magnus von Lagerström,
an officer of the Swedish East India Company,
runner-up to the Dutch
and the British and the French,

scoured Asia for Carl Linnaeus, father of modern
taxonomy (think back to high school biology).

Who itches like me,
bitches like me,
keeps the wind in stitches like me?

I look down through your window. I see you scratch
all through the night even in your sleep.
That flimsy stuff — you call that bark?

Who scratches like you?
Who hatches nothing but words?

Often I think: If you humans could talk,
what would you say?
If you could stand still, would you still stray?

You envy my multiple trunks made of fish scales.
My jacket of gills. My leaves and pennies made of
cats' eyes. My fifty proud species.

Birds draw dreams from my sap as children
suck shakes through a straw.

My prettiness I'm sure of.
The importance of prettiness — not so sure.

I kneel like a doe in the grass.
Then I rise and look down through your window.
Old Man and Old Woman, you drape cloths upon
each other. You bind a plastic tree with light-studded twine.
You think you're thinking of your skin
when actually you're thinking of mine.

So you bring out your dogs to piss on my trunks.
Maybe it's your ability to entertain yourselves
that entertains me.

That high school kid is against
the bylaws. He has to go. I think
I'll help you get rid of him.
He's a danger to me as well.
The other night, walking after
curfew, he caught me raining on

the cocker spaniel that
knows a secret route to freedom
which it takes in a strictly temporary way.

See that guy who's forever popping the ground
switch in the bathroom, who tries so hard to make
himself understood, then realizes people don't
want to understand him, then feels hurt, then
feels relieved because he can forgo all that effort?
Well, he only comes in the Winter and so has
never seen me in bloom.

What he loves about the Swedish Company:
It was preceded by many doomed efforts including
an offer from wealthy, ship-mighty pirates.
Its books weren't cooked — they were burned
to preserve secrecy the charter required.
It couldn't exist till it could be armed to the teeth
to defend itself against other nations' companies that
attacked at the drop of a bicorn hat.

I looked down and in through his dream. He brought
a man home. They fell into bed. His granny was

in the house, so he was nervous. Nevertheless,
they shed their bark and started. Then the old witch

came, unleashing her most magnificent spells.
He too possessed magic and so there ensued

a spectacular duel of dark and light, fire and water,
push and pull. Outdated and exhausted, the witch
crawled away. He crawled onto the man and felt
the man's member like one of my limbs, along his back,
as long as his spine.

Think of ashes and smoke
and know our common language is fire.
Imagine human bodies burnt as fuel.
Imagine trees with memories and senses of humor.
You don't really know what memories are.
Why do you assume we don't have them?

Whose foolish tears are as copious as mine?
Whose wet dreams are as dry?

I can't stop thinking I should be called the Beowulf Tree.

He and his mother and her new hip
practice walking past me on her street.
She knows the name I bear, though
it takes her a day to remember how to say it.

He loves my smooth gray leather bark and multiple trunks.
He thinks of light gray leather pants.
He loves my opposite, simple leaves with their entire margins
and my fruits when they dry to nuts and split along seven lines
and launch their winged seeds.

The seven snake mouths of the Hamburg Hydra
scream/praise Linnaeus's name.
"We are fakes. The Mayor won't make a Thaler off of us
and Linnaeus is to blame."
The thing I love about the Hydra
is its lack of hind legs.
I see Little Boy Linnaeus with his father, looking
under every leaf in his father's garden.
That's what I love about Linnaeus.

It is said that he and his companion fled Hamburg.
What exactly were they afraid of?

With my multiple trunks made from the covering of
an organism from a different taxonomic kingdom,
with my surrealistic jacket, with my leaves and
pennies made from symbolist tropes,
I look down and in through the house on Water Crest Lane.
The writer eats almonds from his palm.

I look down and in through his window.
Night after night he lathers his body,
which he still loves despite its itchy unbecoming heft,
with lotion. Then washes his hands.
Then eats almonds from his palm like a half-tame bird
eating from a child's hand.

3.
Sohlberg: What will the mayor do to us?
Linnaeus: Stitch parts of our bodies into a new
and even more lucrative hoax.
Sohlberg: That seems far-fetched.
Linnaeus: Arrest us on trumped up charges and
see that we meet an ignominious end.
Sohlberg: Perhaps.
Linnaeus: Insure our financial collapse.

4.
I say it to his face. I blow it into his sleeping ear —
making sure it's the right one, for the left
has grown inattentive. The advice is simple and unfeasible.
Leave off the writing. Learn to sculpt me. Do it in wood,
marble and silver — and once a year. papier maché
you can set on fire.

# The Giant

Let's talk measurements to get ahold of this
or to admit it's too big and too small to get ahold of.
Goliath, eleven meters tall with his head,
10.6 without it, has no height at all.
I stand a tad taller than a refrigerator.
My husband's a bit shorter. The David is
seventeen feet tall. The block in which he traveled
from the Alps to Florence was nine *braccia*.
He traveled like a laptop in an airplane's hold.
I picture the marble shaped like a refrigerator.
Cattle pulled it to barges. The Mediterranean
carried it to the Arno. The Arno
passed it on like a runner's baton in
a game of telephone to more cattle.
I'm making this on a 16.2-inch screen.
The Word document is the size
of a standard sheet of printer paper.
It's a glowing white rectangular LCD page.
Briefly blank. If a thing means too much,
handle it over and over. Speak of it till it means less.
Meaning less, it will hurt less.
The white mass Michelangelo worked on
was not a virgin. Two lesser violators
over a period of forty years had hoped to
fuck it up with their tools.
It means something when a piece of writing sits
on high so that its head and hands must swell
to sound right to a reader down below. A bit
of writing. A bit of any act. The effect is obvious

with a facsimile of a body. Less so
with other representations, other theories
of linear perspective. Rock, paper, scissors.
The game brought my husband and me together.
It decided who would be on top and who beneath.
Who would win the bread, who bake it.
Where the gas burners would
emit that unnerving *whoop!*
at the turn of a dial, after a few clicks.
Rock, paper and the tool that cuts, scores, writes.
I cut the questions undersized so they don't
overwhelm the askers, don't distort the answers.
Am I to be the little Michelangelo
of this document? Or the Agostino di Duccio,
patron saint of graspers who get their hands on
a great beauty but cannot get him off?
Will I be the Antonio Rosselino, protector
of studs who make dates but get stood up?
Why do I feel like the quarry in Carrara and not
a block wrested from it? How is *bianco ordinario*
ordinary? Simply by not being superior.
Rock commits all beautiful sins. Paper covers them.
Scissors cut the locks for the lockets and later
cut up the love letters. How many men
and boys have got themselves off
staring mercilessly at this naked sheperd
on a postcard or in an art appreciation textbook?
It is sublime. It's pornographic. It's kitsch.
It's a souvenir of Italy which a philistine aunt
mails to a nephew who admires Goliath.
The number must be  colossal. How many yearners
in earlier centuries developed the pictures in the
darkrooms of their skulls —

clergy, masters and apprentices, laborers who
hauled the giant (the *roccia*, not Goliath),
museum goers and guards. Paper, scissors or rain?
I'm the one who loses sleep
thinking of decades when the rock fetus lay helpless
in a yard of the Duomo workshop — the one
who lives to see what masterpiece
rain would have made
if the marble had lain long enough. Here I stand,
naked as a shepherd who has no reason to be naked —
unless nakedness is needed when one crosses
the line between violence-virgin and slayer.
Chisel, Hammer, Sandpaper. There sits
our home carved in rock. Vellum, pen, ink.
There sprawl the contracts — employment and marriage —
we make and keep. Wood, wheel and muscle.
There march the giant's escorts. Stone, stone, stone.
There whistle the missiles hurled by teenage hooligans
and jealous artists who did not succeed
as the shepherd did; not dead, merely scarred,
this giant lives on. Flint, fur and ice.
There wags Michelangelo's giant head
at 26 and at 80. "I never acted on my loves,"
he said. Did he lie to preserve his liberty
and reputation? It's as possible as the David is
famous. Affection, security, time.
All may break and cover and cut the libido.
The Old Man may well have told the truth.
(Would Savonarola have burned Buonarroti
and Cavalieri if they had proved their passion was chaste?)
Now I am the world's largest Frigidaire stranded
in the middle of Nebraska, determined
to get to the Republic that kicked the Medicis out.

I am upright and suspended lest my feet touch the
ground. Not angels, but the roughest cowboys
of the Renaissance keep me aloft. Not the Divine Will,
but greased beams on the ground
are the authors of my progress. Forty days
of our shy, then less and less shy dates.
Forty awkward nights. Once a jammed finger,
the least of injuries, brought love-making to a halt.
One night after closing, tattooed numbers appeared
above the suicidal veins of a wrist.
Soon they were gone, licked off by a hard tongue,
like the darkness in the corner erased by dawn.
Forty days on the Ocean of Deception.
Forty nights of coming clean.
I can never say enough about the vandalism
that followed me from the workshop
to the Palace of Lords. Stone on stone violence.
Stones that aimed to bruise me into another race,
Purple or Black. The first thrower may well
have been without sin. Those he inspired were not.
Those lifeless grenades weren't thrown at all.
It was my gravity that pulled them.
They were two or three in number.
They were a deluge. Rain came and drenched
the rock-trees, and the rock-trees shook like
wet dogs flinging ripe rock fruit.
They were harbingers of asteroids that will chasten
humanity once and for all.
They were meant to be pebbles tossed at
a lover's window, but there was no glass and no
pebbles were to be had, not even for love or money.
Throwing stones at eight tons of marble
is like throwing flowers at a condemned bride

of Christ. They had no other speech
to warn me against my pride. I didn't listen
and so let them bear me through
the city streets, a Godzilla saint, and install
me on the cathedral roof, which I brought
down on the heads of all present,
making such a jumble of organic and
inorganic limbs — and architecture —
that the subsequent restoration resulted in
wrong and monstrous features.
The two-toothed chisel
the artist handled like a pro handles her mouth, it
was real. The three-toothed chisel
he compared to the trinity, also real.
The flat chisels he scorned, wouldn't have
scorned him. The hand-drill and bow
that cut a mockery of sight
in the David's head, they were fiddle and bow
for the Devil of the Dead. One night he told
Tommaso "My claim that I liberate
figures already in rocky existence —
it's showmanship. Its salesmanship."
Maybe the Old Man didn't lie. Maybe he,
like my husband, was in love with
the Ken-Doll beauty of the human male —
every inch but the ridiculous
genitalia, Jabba the Hutt before he got fat.
Suddenly the lights go out in the gallery.
Every last gawker but me freezes
like the kings on a chessboard.
David clambers down from his pedestal,
shrinking and turning to flesh
as he nears the floor. He sits,

shakes his head, dislodging a bad dream
and pulls on thick woolen socks.
He drops his head in my lap
and looks up with sparkling eyes.
How tired he was of glaring
and how cold his feet had been. He talks
of the man who stole one of his noses.
And the highly dedicated, some would say
radical mohel, who cut off the skin
that grew back overnight like a worm cut in two.
I say, "In junior high school, in the 70s…"
"Which 70s?" he asks. "The 1970s."
"Ah, I remember them." "Suddenly
I knew I was in love with my best friend.
Something rose up and surrounded me. Not
fear, but a kind of listening. Then one night
I heard a voice from my parents' TV.
A middle-aged man had come out to
a woman who wanted to marry him.
She wanted to know: Did he not see the beauty
of women? 'Oh, yes. When I look at
Botticelli's Venus I see a beautiful work of art.
But when I look at Michelangelo's David,
my heart beats urgently,
and everything but that body gets blurry.'
I'd give a lot to know what show my parents were
watching that night and if they sensed
the effort of my ears and the
stopping of my heart in the next room."
"You know I'm straight," David apologizes.
I smile. We know what we owe each other
and are grateful. The dome
opens like a tulip.